SUBMARINES &
SHIPS

RICHARD HUMBLE

Viking

Acknowledgments

The publishers would like to thank Jonathan Adams, who illustrated the four see-through scenes and the heading icons; Gerald Wood, who illustrated the cover; and the organizations and individuals who have given their permission to reproduce the pictures in this book:

Ancient Art & Architecture Collection/Ronald Sheridan: 9.
Archiv fur Kunst und Geschichte/Erich Lessing: 7, 42 left.
Bibliotheque Nationale, Paris: 15.
Bridgeman Art Library/Lambeth Palace Library: 21 top left, /
National Maritime Museum: 26 top, /Bonhams, London: 29 top.
The British Library: 19 (Royal 10e iv f19). **Christie's Images:** 27 bottom.
Department of Defense, Still Media Records Center/Gallagher Phan: 45.
Mary Evans Picture Library: 34, 41.
Michael Holford: 4, /British Museum: 6, /Museum vor Volkekunde, Munich: 11, /
Musee de Bayeux: 13, /Science Museum: 21 bottom left, /Science Museum: 21 right, /
Science Museum: 22.
Robert Hunt Library: 42 right, 43 bottom.
Richard Hunter: 36. **Imperial War Museum:** 43 top.
Kon-Tiki Museum, Oslo: 5. **National Maritime Museum, Antwerp:** 23.
National Maritime Museum, London: 25, 26 bottom, 27 top, 29 bottom.
Colin Martin: 24 top right. **The Mary Rose Trust:** 24 top left.
Photographie Giraudon/Reims Cathedral: 18.
Reed International Books Ltd/Mark R. Wallis: 30.
S.S. Great Britain/S.W.P.A: 31.
T.R.H./U.S. Navy: 35. **U.S. Navy**/E.J. Bonner: 39.
Werner Forman Archive/Statens Historiska Museum, Stockholm: 12.

Illustrators:
Jonathan Adams: 8–9, 16–17, 32–33, 40–41, heading icons.
Peter Bull Art: all maps.
Bill Donohoe: 4 bottom, 5, 34.
Nick Hewetson: 6–7, 14, 23 middle right, 43 bottom right, 46–47.
Christian Hook: 4 top left, 10–11 (both).
Jonathon Potter: 22, 30–31, 35, 44–45 (both).
Tony Townsend: 13 (bottom right), 15, 18, 21, 23 bottom, 28 top left, 29,
31 bottom right, 42–43 (main picture).
Paul Weston: 19, 27, 38–39 (both).
Gerald Wood: Cover, 12–13 (main picture), 20, 24, 25,
28 bottom, 36–37 (both).

VIKING
Published by the Penguin Group
Penguin Putnam Inc., 375 Hudson Street, New York, New York 10014, U.S.A.
Penguin Books Ltd, 27 Wrights Lane, London W8 5TZ, England
Penguin Books Australia Ltd, Ringwood, Victoria, Australia
Penguin Books Canada Ltd, 10 Alcorn Avenue, Toronto, Ontario, Canada M4V 3B2
Penguin Books (N.Z.) Ltd, 182–190 Wairau Road, Auckland 10, New Zealand

Penguin Books Ltd, Registered Offices: Harmondsworth, Middlesex, England

First published in Great Britain by Hamlyn Children's Books, 1995
First published in the United States of America by Viking,
a member of Penguin Putnam Inc., 1997

1   3   5   7   9   10   8   6   4   2

Library of Congress Catalog Card Number: 96-61760

ISBN 0-670-86778-0

Printed in Belgium

CONTENTS

THE FIRST BOATS

Coracles (above) are very simple boats made from animal skins stretched over a bowl-shaped framework. They are very light and easy to carry. Dugout canoes (top right) were first made about 10,000 years ago, in the Stone Age. They are made by hollowing out a log, or sometimes by burning the center of the log away.

Rafts are floating platforms made by tying logs together side by side. Rafts can carry more passengers than dugout canoes, but are less stable and harder to paddle and steer.

Long ago, before the first written records, early humans learned to use floating materials such as logs, bundles of reeds, and inflated animal skins to travel along rivers and across lakes. Five thousand years ago, people of the great civilizations of Egypt and Sumer built the first sail-powered ships and ventured into the open sea. These first simple boats were the ancestors of the great sailing ships and luxury liners that sail the oceans today.

THE FIRST BOATS

Boat-building is an ancient and important craft. It enabled people to travel without being hindered by rivers and lakes, to fish for food, and to make short voyages out to sea. Prehistoric boat-building probably began with rafts (platforms of logs tied together with rope) and coracles (wooden frames covered with animal skins). They are both paddled, because neither is big enough to carry a mast and be sailed. Coracles were probably first used for fishing in rivers and lakes, and are still used in several countries today.

This tomb-carving from about 2400 B.C. shows Egyptian shipbuilders at work. They are using adzes (a kind of ax) and chisels to smooth the planking of the ship's hollow hull. The hull planks were fastened together with wooden pegs.

REED BOATS

The earliest seagoing boats were built around 3000 B.C. by the river peoples of Egypt, Sumer (now southern Iraq), and Mohenjo-Daro (Pakistan). These countries did not have trees to use for building large boats, but their rivers were densely fringed with papyrus reeds.

4

Egyptian carvings from 5,000 years ago show boat builders expertly tying reeds into stiff bundles. These were then lashed together to form a hull curved upward at the bow (front) and stern (back). Small boats were driven and steered by paddles. Bigger ones were steered by large oars at the stern, but carried a sail made of a square piece of cloth on a two-legged mast to catch tailwinds.

TRADING BY SEA

The Sumerians and Egyptians soon began to use these ships for trade. This was because traveling by sea was faster than traveling by land. Although few ships were seaworthy enough to venture far from land, the Egyptians were soon busy trading along the Mediterranean coast between the mouth of the Nile river and Lebanon. It was from Lebanon that Egypt imported cedar wood to build bigger and better ships.

THE OLDEST KNOWN SHIP

The Egyptians used the imported Lebanon cedar to build the oldest known ship still in existence today. It was used only once, for the funeral of Pharaoh Khufu (Cheops), builder of the Great Pyramid, who ruled Egypt around 2600 B.C.

This graceful craft is 167 feet long, and was rowed by 10 oars. It was taken apart and buried with the dead pharaoh. Some 4,500 years later, archaeologists discovered the ship and fitted together its 1,200 planks—making it the world's oldest modeling kit!

Thor Heyerdahl's ship Ra, *made of papyrus reeds. Six years after his voyage on the* Ra, *Heyerdahl sailed a Sumerian-type reed ship, called* Tigris, *around Africa from Iraq to Somalia: a voyage of 4,185 miles in 144 days.*

The last voyage of a dead pharaoh. Although built with great craftsmanship, the elegant funeral ships of ancient Egypt were designed only for the calm waters of the Nile river, not for voyages on the open sea.

VOYAGE OF THE *RA*

Modern experiments have proved that some Sumerian and Egyptian reed ships were actually capable of making long voyages on the open sea. In 1970, using the skills of African and South American peoples who still build reed boats, Norwegian explorer Thor Heyerdahl built a reed ship 59 feet long and 20 feet wide. Heyerdahl's crew sailed this ship, named *Ra* after the Egyptian sun god, across the Atlantic Ocean. Setting out from Morocco in North Africa, *Ra* reached Barbados in the West Indies in 57 days.

FLEETS OF THE PHARAOHS

T he Egyptian empire was the world's first sea power, building ships for both trade and war. The merchant ships sailed the seas to bring home the riches of East Africa, while the fighting ships won important battles at sea.

By the time of the Egyptian "Middle Kingdom" (about 1991–1786 B.C.), ships and boats were so important in the life of Egypt that models of them were buried with the dead. The Egyptians believed that the dead would be able to use them in an afterlife. This model of an Egyptian sailing boat dates from about 1800 B.C.

SHIPS FOR WAR OR PEACE

About a hundred years after the burial of Khufu's funeral ship, the pharaoh Sahure sent a fleet of eight troop-carrying ships to attack the coast of Syria. To celebrate the success of the mission, the pharoah built a victory monument that was decorated with pictures of his ships. It clearly shows vessels which could carry cargo as well as troops. They could be rowed or sailed, with seven oars on each side. The two-legged mast carried a single square sail, and was lowered backward onto a tall cradle when the ship was being rowed. There were six steering oars at the stern, three on each side.

QUEEN HATSHEPSUT'S FLEET

The powerful Queen Hatshepsut ruled Egypt from 1503–1482 B.C. Her most famous monument is to a sea voyage not of war but of peace. It shows ships from a trading fleet which sailed down the Red Sea to the "Land of Punt" (probably modern Somalia, in East Africa). Each ship was much bigger than Sahure's warships, with twice as many oars (14 on each side).

The hull was built up from a central backbone called a keel, which does not seem to have been a feature of earlier Egyptian ships. The keel gave the ship increased strength, and rose at either end to form a high bow and a gracefully curved stern. It supported a single fixed mast that had replaced the two-legged collapsible mast of Sahure's ships.

This map shows the seas cruised by the seagoing reed ships of Sumer and the reed and wooden ships of Egypt: the Mediterranean and Red Seas, and south to the Indian Ocean and the coast of East Africa.

Egypt
Sumer
East Africa
INDIAN OCEAN

DECK BEAMS AND RIGGING

Queen Hatshepsut's ships also had wooden beams across them, supporting the deck and bracing the sides of the ship together. This use of beams shows that there were probably large cargo holds below deck, and that these vessels were broader and stronger than earlier Egyptian ships. They were probably between 95 and 105 feet long, judging by the number of oars.

In addition to being stronger and more seaworthy, Queen Hatshepsut's ships were probably much easier to sail than those of Sahure's fleet. Details of their rigging clearly show ropes that could be used for swinging the sail to catch changes in the wind direction.

RAMESSES III

Egypt's last great warrior pharaoh was Ramesses III (1198–1166 B.C.). During his reign, Egypt was attacked by enemies whom the Egyptians called the "people from the sea." These were probably tribes driven south from Crete. Ramesses defeated them on land and at sea.

SEA BATTLES

Ramesses' tomb at Medinet Habu has the first known pictures of a sea battle. It shows a type of warship which would be used in sea battles for almost 3,000 years to come: war galleys, built solely for fighting.

Galleys were narrow, lightly built ships that had both sails and oars. They were sailed when looking for the enemy fleet, but rowed into battle. Their keel extended forward to form a pointed ram strengthened with a heavy bronze animal head for smashing holes in enemy ships. When the galley had managed to hit an enemy ship, the rowers would then back the galley away before attacking the next ship. The galleys of Ramesses III also carried soldiers for boarding and capturing enemy vessels.

This relief from Queen Hatshepsut's tomb shows a cargo-carrying ship from the trading fleet she sent to the East African "Land of Punt."

This reconstruction of one of the war galleys of Ramesses III shows its single fixed mast and the forward-jutting ram for smashing and sinking enemy ships in battle. The galleys each had a single steering oar.

7

GREECE AND ROME

After the decline of the Egyptian empire, Phoenicia (now part of Syria) and Greece emerged as the next great sea powers. However, they in turn were eclipsed by the might of the Romans.

GALLEYS

The Phoenicians' rise to power began around 1100 B.C. They protected their merchant fleets with war galleys. So did their rivals in southern Europe, the city-states of Greece. The first Greek galleys had just one bank, or row, of oars on each side. Each oar was about 40 feet long. By the fifth century B.C., the trireme (above right), rowed by three banks, was the backbone of the Greek fleet.

ROME'S BATTLE FLEETS

Eventually, the city of Rome became the most powerful state in the northern Mediterranean. But when Rome tried to take control of Sicily, it was challenged by the sea-trading empire of Carthage, which the Phoenicians had founded in North Africa. Rome defeated Carthage in a series of sea battles (264–241 B.C.), using war galleys that were even bigger than the Greek triremes. Roman galleys carried a weighted drawbridge called a "corvus," or crow. This was dropped onto enemy decks so that the Roman soldiers could charge across and capture the ship.

ROMAN MERCHANT SHIPS

By the end of the first century B.C., Rome's power had spread from one end of the Mediterranean to the other. The Roman empire depended on trade for its prosperity. Hundreds of merchant ships were constantly at sea. Apart from the tons of grain needed to feed all the citizens of the empire, the ships carried oil and wine in earthenware jars, thousands of wild animals from Asia and Africa, and luxury goods from Asia.

1 **Bow mast**
2 **Mainmast with mainsail brailed (pulled up to yard)**
3 **Cargo hatches**
4 **Stern deckhouse with cabins**
5 **Steering oar**
6 **Grain storage in hold**
7 **Cargo of marble blocks**

SQUARE SAIL AND ARTEMON

We know what Roman merchant ships looked like from pictures on monuments and coins. The hull was deep and rounded. The curving stern-post rose high and was carved into a graceful goose head, which was painted or gilded. The mainmast carried a large square sail, and an angled bow mast carried a smaller sail called an "artemon." The ship was steered by twin steering oars linked by a bar controlled by a helmsman. The biggest of these ships were at least 164 feet long, and over 43 feet from the deck to the bottom of the hold.

8   **Crossbeams supporting deck**
9   **Cargo of wine in jars (*amphorae*)**
10 **Slaves unloading grain in sacks**
11 **Factory making *amphorae***
12 **Animal escaping from cage**

In this picture from a Roman floor mosaic, a fisherman is about to cast his anchor so that his boat doesn't drift while he fishes. The basic shape of the anchor has remained unchanged for hundreds of years.

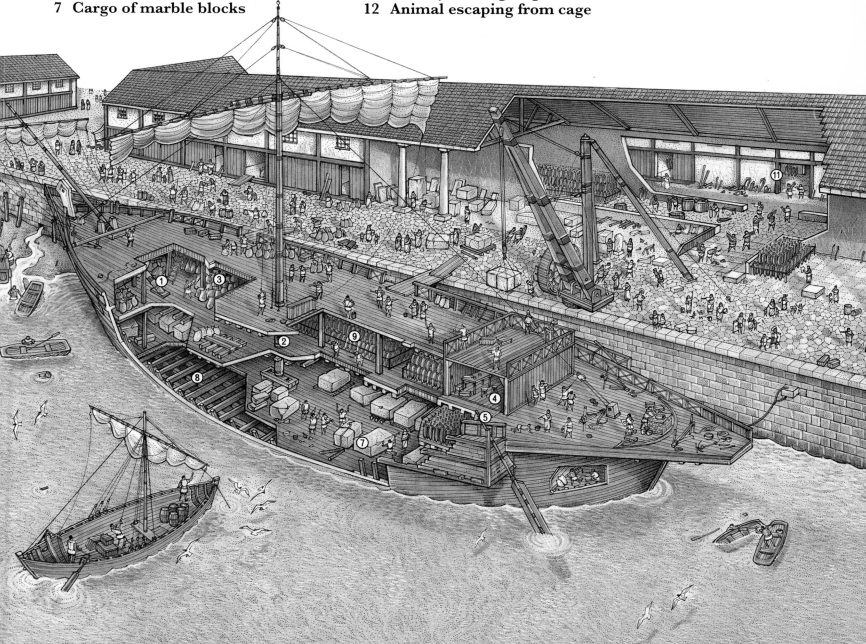

The first human settlers of the islands of the Pacific Ocean—the world's biggest sea—made amazing voyages in their canoes. The Marquesas Islands are at the center of the map. Also shown is the proposed route of the South American balsa rafts.

B etween about 100 B.C. and A.D. 200, while the Roman Empire was at the peak of its power, the first human settlement of the Pacific islands was beginning on the other side of the world.

EAST TO THE MARQUESAS

The first Pacific voyages were made by people from mainland Asia. They sailed east in large canoes, seeking new lands in which to live. Pottery relics indicate that they had reached the hundreds of islands between New Guinea and Samoa as early as 1100 B.C. By about A.D. 300, they had reached the Marquesas Islands, over 1,860 miles east of Samoa. From there they made more incredible voyages, northwest to Hawaii and southwest to New Zealand.

The fast-sailing "double canoe" of the Pacific was a type known today as the catamaran. A cross between a simple canoe and a raft, it was built by connecting two canoe-shaped hulls with a central platform.

THE "DOUBLE CANOE"

The Hawaiian name for the craft that first conquered the Pacific was *wa'a kaulua*, the "double canoe." It consisted of two curving hulls joined by a platform, with one or more masts carrying tall sails. The sails were made of braided pandanus leaves, and were hooked like crab claws. Europeans exploring the Pacific islands in the 18th century reported that the biggest *wa'a kaulua* were over 98 feet long, and could carry 50 or more people. The *wa'a kaulua* was built of wood, with hollowed tree trunks forming the undersides of the twin hulls.

Though a fast sailer, the *wa'a kaulua* was light enough to be driven by paddles in calm weather, and was steered by a large paddle at the stern.

Asia

Hawaiian Islands

PACIFIC OCEAN

New Guinea

Balsa rafts

Polynesia

Peru

New Zealand

THE LEGEND OF TIKI

The islanders of southern Polynesia, around Tahiti, trace their origins to the god-king Tiki. Tiki is said to have brought the first Polynesians to the islands, sailing not from the west (Asia) but from the east, from "a big country beyond the sea." We now think this "country" was South America. Plants found on some South Pacific islands that are native to South America, not the islands, seem to bear out this theory.

A South American legend tells of another god-king, Kon-Tiki, or "Sun-Tiki." His people had been driven from the city of Tiahuanaco, in the country we now call Bolivia, around A.D. 500. According to legend, Kon-Tiki and his people reached the Pacific coast and sailed across the sea.

ON RAFTS OF BALSA

We know that the peoples who lived in the countries we now call Peru and Bolivia were ocean voyagers. Unlike the Pacific islanders, they used rafts instead of canoes. These were made of balsa logs and had square sails. It was once thought that the spongy balsa logs would have become sodden with water, sinking in mid-ocean long before the people reached the South Pacific islands. However, researchers now believe Kon-Tiki's people could have made the 4,500 mile journey to Polynesia.

Oceangoing rafts, built of large balsa-wood logs, probably sailed westward across the Pacific from the South American coast.

When you are on the ocean you cannot see any islands. Only the things we bring with us help us to survive. We act together. That is all I have to say. Remember, all of you, and we will see that place we are going to.

—— *Mau Piailug, canoe sailing master* ——

TRIUMPH OF THE *KON-TIKI*

In 1947, Thor Heyerdahl set out to prove that South Americans could have colonized the Pacific Islands. He built the *Kon-Tiki*, a balsa-log raft, and sailed it from Peru to Polynesia—4,290 miles—in 101 days. There, on a Pacific island, Heyerdahl planted a coconut palm brought from South America, to prove that such a voyage could have been made.

RELEARNING TO SAIL

More proof came in 1976 when a replica of an ancient *wa'a kaulua*, named *Hokule'a*, sailed from Hawaii. Navigating by the stars, the *Hokule'a* reached Tahiti, 2,976 miles to the south. During the 35-day voyage her crew rediscovered some of the sailing skills used by the Pacific's first conquerors.

This wooden figure was carved in the Solomon Islands in the 19th century to decorate the prow (front) of a canoe. The figure was the craftsman's way of remembering his ocean-crossing ancestors, and was believed to protect the canoe from evil spirits.

11

VIKING SHIPS

A silver coin made in Denmark and found in Sweden shows a Viking longship with its sail partly lowered.

This busy scene at a Viking port shows cargo and livestock being unloaded from knorrs (merchant ships). In the background is a fighting drakkar under sail.

After the fall of the Roman empire in the fifth century A.D., the next advance in European shipbuilding took place in northern waters. This was the construction of tough, seaworthy "longships."

THE FIRST LONGSHIPS

The first longships were used by the Angles and Saxons. They rowed rather than sailed these ships, which were open to the sea. One such longship was discovered in a Danish peat bog. The ship was built of oak planks, with positions for 15 oars on each side. It was steered by an oar on the right-hand side of the ship. This side was known as the "steering board," which is the origin of the modern word, "starboard."

THE VIKING DRAKKARS

The real masters of the longship were the Vikings. Between about A.D. 800 and 1000, the Viking "drakkars" or "dragon ships" of Norway, Sweden, and Denmark were the terror of Europe. Several have survived, buried in Viking funeral mounds.

Drakkars were designed to be sailed or rowed. When the ship approached land, or when it needed to maneuver carefully, the mast and sail were lowered and the crew rowed. The great *Ormr inn langi* or "Long Serpent," owned by King Olaf Tryggvason of Norway, is said to have had as many as 34 oars on each side.

ASHORE AND AFLOAT

Viking ships did not sit deep in the water, and could be hauled ashore. When they carried horses or other livestock, the animals could easily be landed by tipping the ship over to one side. Although the planks of the hull were nailed together, they were tied to the ribs with spruce roots. This meant the ship was very flexible and would not be easily damaged by the pounding of heavy waves.

When sailing, the Vikings did not have to rely on tailwinds. If they wanted to sail at an angle to the wind, they kept the sail stretched open with a piece of wood called a bracing spar, or *beiti-ass*. The bottom timber of the Viking ship, the keel, helped the ship to keep a straight course.

CARGO-CARRYING KNORRS

The Vikings were great traders and colonists, eager to find new markets for their goods and new lands in which to settle. But little is known about their cargo ships, which they called "knorrs." The knorr was developed from the drakkar but was broader and had higher sides to protect its stacks of cargo. Knorrs were used to carry wood to the treeless Norse colonies on Iceland and Greenland, and to bring back bales of seal and polar bear fur.

In about A.D. 986, a knorr owned by a merchant seaman named Bjarni sailed for the new colony of Greenland. Bjarni was blown far off course by bad weather, only reaching Greenland after sighting a strange new land to the southwest. Later, Leif Eriksson, the son of Greenland's ruler, bought Bjarni's knorr and became the first European to sail down the coast of Labrador to Newfoundland. He had reached North America over 500 years before Christopher Columbus.

These cross-sections of ships, based on archaeological finds, show how Viking ships developed. The top two ships do not have a keel. The third ship has a simple keel and a wider hull. The fourth vessel, known as the Oseberg ship, is the first Viking ship known to have had a mast. The bottom diagram shows the Gokstad ship, which had a more substantial keel and a support for the mast.

The longship remained the favorite type of ship in northern Europe for several hundred years. This scene from the Bayeux Tapestry shows Normans building longship transports for the invasion of England in A.D. 1066.

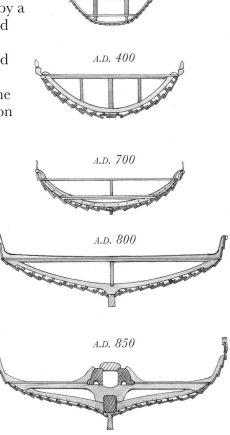

A.D. 300

A.D. 400

A.D. 700

A.D. 800

A.D. 850

13

The great years of Viking and Arab seafaring overlapped. Throughout the Middle Ages, Arab sailors ruled the seas from Africa to Southeast Asia. Although their ships rarely met, the Vikings and Arabs traded together, exchanging goods and slaves.

Chinese

Vikings

Arabs

An Arab boum under full sail, showing the stern rudder and cargo hold beneath the deck. The smell below deck was rancid, because the ship's planks were swabbed regularly with vegetable oil.

In the seventh and eighth centuries A.D., the Arabs conquered the Persian empire, most of the Greek-speaking eastern Roman empire, the whole coast of North Africa, and Spain. The Arabs were great sailors as well as outstanding warriors. By A.D. 1000, while Greenland's Vikings were voyaging west to North America, Arab navigators were sailing to the East Indies and China.

ARABIAN SHIPS

Arab ships could not have been more different from those of the Vikings. The overlapping planks of Viking hulls were stoutly nailed together, while the smooth hulls of Arab ships were built with their planks laid edge to edge. These planks were then stitched together with hundreds of miles of cord made from coir, or coconut fiber. Arab shipbuilders learned that if the coir was regularly soaked with vegetable oil, a ship would last from six to ten times longer than a ship whose timbers were fastened with iron nails.

Like Egypt, Arabia did not have wood suitable for shipbuilding. So lumber was one of the first cargoes brought home by Arab traders. The Egyptians had sailed only 186 miles between the Nile and Lebanon, but the Arabs made voyages of more than 930 miles across the Arabian Sea to bring back teak wood from the forests of India.

MASTS AND SAILS

The Arabs were great scientists in every subject from astronomy to medicine. They used these skills in navigation and shipbuilding. They were the first known seafarers to fit their ships with two masts.

Instead of the traditional square sail, the Arabs favored triangular or "lateen" sails. The sails were arranged or "rigged" along the line of the ship's keel instead of across it. They included a small triangular "jib" at the ship's bow, which is still used in sailing craft today. The Arabs found that a ship rigged like this could sail closer to the wind (see below), and make progress even when the wind did not blow from behind.

RUDDERS

The Arabs were among the first sailors to fit their ships with rudders for steering. The hinged rudder, hung on stout pins fitted to the ship's stern-post, was much better for controlling a ship's direction than a steering oar. This was one of the most important improvements made to ships during the Middle Ages.

BOUM

The most famous type of ocean-going Arab ship was the boum, 82 feet or more long. The posts at its bow and stern were straight, and it carried large triangular sails on two masts, and a jib. Almost 400 miles of coir was used on the hull of a boum. The fiber was threaded and knotted through some 20,000 holes that had been slowly hand-drilled through the hard teak wood.

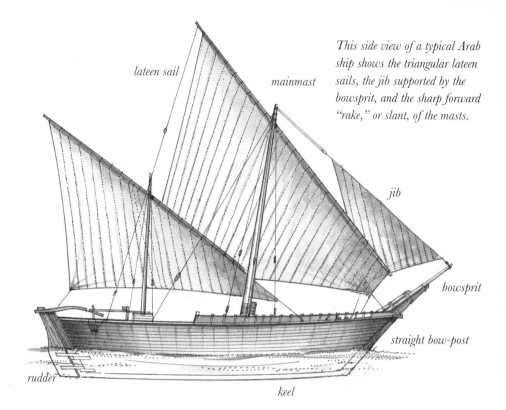

lateen sail *mainmast* *jib* *bowsprit* *straight bow-post* *rudder* *keel*

This side view of a typical Arab ship shows the triangular lateen sails, the jib supported by the bowsprit, and the sharp forward "rake," or slant, of the masts.

RICHES OF THE EAST

Using their great skills and ships like the boum, the Arabs sailed over 2,480 miles down the East African coast, and 3,720 miles around the coast of India to the East Indies. By the 13th century A.D., Arab ships were sailing as far as China, another 1,550 miles farther north. The wealth of this huge sea-trading empire —silks and spices, jewels and porcelain—remained under Arab control for the next 300 years.

The sharply angled posts at the bow and stern stand out in this 13th-century picture of an Arab ship. Notice the efficient-looking four-pronged anchor hanging from the bow.

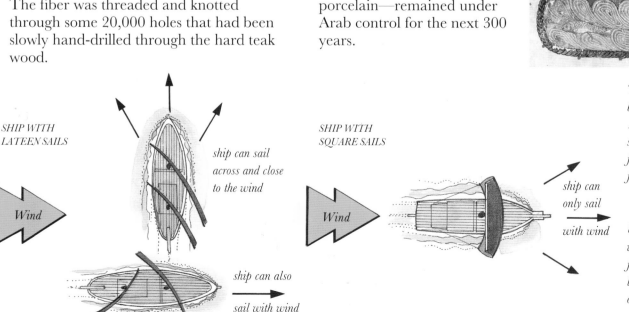

SHIP WITH LATEEN SAILS

Wind

ship can sail across and close to the wind

ship can also sail with wind

SHIP WITH SQUARE SAILS

Wind

ship can only sail with wind

Unlike the square sail (left), which depends on tailwinds, fore-and-aft lateen sails (far left) allow a ship to "reach," or sail across the wind, as well as sail with it.

15

GIANTS OF THE SEA

The Chinese were skilled navigators. We know that by the 12th century they were using magnetic compasses (above right) to chart their courses.

The Arabs who reached the Far East were among the first western people to see the huge trading junks of the Chinese. Junks were the biggest ships in the world at that time.

We shall tell you first of the ships in which merchants trading with India make their voyages. They are built of spruce and fir. They have one deck; and above this, in most ships, are at least 60 cabins, each of which can comfortably accommodate one merchant.

— *Marco Polo* —

AMAZING SHIPS

The huge Chinese vessels—built to carry passengers as well as cargo—clearly amazed Venetian explorer Marco Polo in the 13th century. The *pechili* junks were 180 feet long and 30 feet across. A junk's hull was made of two thicknesses of planks nailed together, and had a flat bottom. Marco noted another novelty: Chinese ships carried only one "steering oar"—actually a rudder at the stern.

MASTS AND SAILS

The Chinese had discovered that ships sail far better with more than one mast. Chinese ships had four masts, and carried two extra ones that could be raised when needed. The sails were square, and woven of stout matting instead of cloth. The Chinese stiffened the sails with bamboo slats. The slats kept the sails stretched, and made them more efficient at catching even the lightest winds.

WATERTIGHT COMPARTMENTS

Another remarkable feature of China's big junks was their hulls. These were divided into 14 watertight sections by strong walls called bulkheads. If the ship leaked or hit a rock, only one or two sections would be flooded instead of the whole ship. It was centuries before European ships were designed with bulkheads.

1 **Hull made of two layers of planks**
2 **Watertight bulkheads**
3 **Flat bottom**
4 **Tiller (bar for turning rudder)**
5 **Rudder**
6 **Cargo of baskets of pepper**
7 **Bamboo slats**
8 **Crew's quarters**

This large ocean-going junk is typical of those seen by Marco Polo when he traveled throughout China around 1275–95. Marco, who had traveled from Venice, one of Europe's most powerful trading nations, wrote in great detail about the ships he saw.

THE EUROPEAN COG

This golden reliquary from 15th-century France shows a "nef." The nef was a bigger form of the cog, but still had a single mast and sail, plus fore- and sterncastles.

This diagram shows how a cog's winch, called a windlass, could be used for unloading cargo, as well as for raising and lowering the sail and anchor. The yard, from which the sail would hang, is being used like the boom of a crane.

The longship did not vanish with the end of the Viking era in the 11th century. The only real change over the next 150 years was that towers were built at its bow and stern. These towers were called "forecastles" and "sterncastles," and carried soldiers during wartime. But by the middle of the 13th century a new type of ship was emerging: the sturdy cog.

THE HANSEATIC LEAGUE

The years between about 1150 and 1250 saw the growth of wealthy German trading ports like Hamburg, Lübeck, Stralsund, and Rostock. To protect and extend their growing trade on the North and Baltic seas, they banded together to form the Hanseatic League. ("Hansa" meant a group or company of allies.) Each of the League's biggest trading cities had its own official seal, which most chose to decorate with a picture of a ship. By the 1240s, nearly all these seals (above right) were showing the same type of ship, which is best known as the "Hansa cog."

THE END OF THE LONGSHIP

In pictures on seals and in manuscripts, it is clear that the cog had a hull of overlapping planks and a single square sail. However, in no other way was it like the old longships. The cog was shorter, broader, and deeper. It had straight bow- and stern-posts rising from a straight keel. The hull was not open but had a deck over it. And the biggest change was that the cog had a hinged rudder, not a steering oar. Probably by chance, the Hanseatic shipbuilders had used many features of the Arab boum—which was almost unknown to 13th-century German seamen.

THE COG OF BREMEN

Historians argued for many years about the size of cogs, and exactly how they were built. Then, in 1962, a cog was found buried deep in the mud near the old German seaport of Bremen. The condition of its timbers showed that this had been a brand-new ship. It had not even been finished when it was swept away in a flood and sunk, probably around 1380.

Built of oak planks, the Bremen cog is 77 feet long. The boat's displacement, or weight in the water, would have been about 152 tons. Rising above the main deck the boat has a sterncastle supporting a heavy winch, called a windlass. This was used to raise and lower the sail and anchor, to hoist cargo in and out of the hold, and also to "trim" the sail—swinging it to and fro to catch as much wind as possible.

DESIGNED FOR BEACHING

On each side of the Bremen cog, the three lowest planks of the hull were fixed edge to edge, giving the ship a very strong bottom. The cog's straight keel and stout bottom timbers enabled it to be beached. This meant it could deliver goods to places where there were no harbors or docks at which to load and unload. The ship would then float off safely on the next high tide.

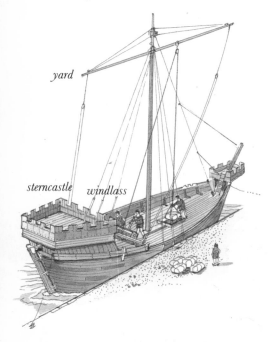

yard

sterncastle windlass

CARGOES OF THE NORTH

Five stout beams run across the Bremen cog from side to side, their ends sticking out through the side planking. These beams support the deck, under which lies the deep cargo hold.

Many tough little ships like the Bremen cog carried the goods on which the trade of medieval Europe depended: corn, wine, wool, livestock, timber, iron, and pitch. It was during this time (about 1200–1400) that ships began to be measured by the number of barrels or "tuns" they could carry as cargo. This is the origin of the word "tonnage," still used to measure the weight of ships today, and of the modern word "ton."

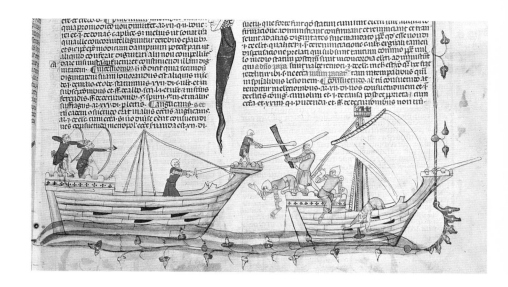

This 14th-century manuscript shows a battle between cogs, both of which have forecastles and sterncastles. Archers are shooting from the high sterncastle of the ship on the left.

The strong, straight keel and deep rounded hull of a cog were ideal for beaching the ship where there was no convenient harbor for loading and unloading cargo or repairing the ship. Props on either side kept the ship upright until the tide floated it off again.

OCEAN-CROSSING CARAVELS

Crewmen prepare to set the mainsail of a busy caravel. On deck, the navigator is using a cross-staff to find the ship's position from the height of the sun. This caravel also has an early gun mounted on its rail.

The caravel was small, fast, and seaworthy—an ideal ship for making long ocean voyages. A blend of Mediterranean and northern European designs, the caravel made it possible for European adventurers to explore the Atlantic and Indian Oceans.

CLINKER VERSUS CARVEL

By 1400, ships in Europe had been built with overlapping planks (a method called clinker-building) for over a thousand years. But Mediterranean seamen had found a better way of building ships. In the 15th century this new method, called "carvel-building" (from the word *caravel*), spread to seafaring countries along Europe's Atlantic coast.

Ships built carvel-style had a smooth hull. The planks were laid edge to edge over strong frames attached to the keel. This method enabled ships to be bigger and stronger than clinker-built ones. The smooth plank skin also helped carvel-built ships sail better and faster.

SQUARE SAILS OR LATEEN?

The caravel was a small ship. It was clearly developed from Portuguese oceangoing fishing boats designed for the Atlantic. Pictures of caravels show that they were a mix of old and new. They had a hinged rudder like cogs, but a square stern instead of a pointed one. They had a low rounded bow, and were rigged with two masts and lateen sails like Arab ships. They also carried a third mast in the stern: a mizzenmast.

Cabot and others

Columbus and others

Da Gama and others

Magellan and Del Cano

Some of the ocean routes explored by caravels and other ships between 1450 and 1600, including Magellan and Del Cano's around-the-world voyage.

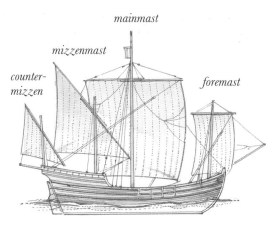

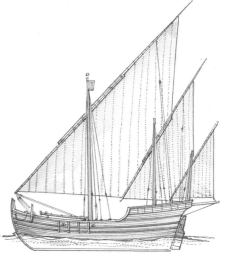

On their long voyages, the sailors of Portugal and Spain discovered that the caravel could be rigged with either lateen or square sails, or better still a combination of both. This mixture of rigs enabled the ship to tack (zigzag) into the wind, or sail powerfully before a tailwind.

REACHING OUT FOR INDIA

Supported by Prince Henry "The Navigator" (1394–1460), Portuguese caravels began sailing farther and farther down the unexplored west coast of Africa. By 1460, they were rounding Africa's western bulge and bringing back cargoes of African gold, ivory, and slaves.

Then, in 1488, Bartholomew Diaz sailed even farther south, around the Cape of Good Hope and into the Indian Ocean. Ten years later, Vasco da Gama led the first Portuguese trading fleet on the long voyage around Africa to India and back. The caravel brought the riches of the Indies within the reach of European traders for the first time.

THE FAMOUS *NIÑA*

The most famous caravel was the *Niña*. About 66 feet long and carrying about 66 tons of stores and cargo, it was one of three ships used by Christopher Columbus during his first crossing of the Atlantic in 1492. After his flagship, the *Santa Maria*, was wrecked, the great explorer sailed back to Spain in the *Niña*.

The ship's navigator recorded the ship's course using a traverse board (right). Every half an hour, a peg was put in a hole corresponding to the direction the ship was sailing. When he had several recordings, the navigator could then "plot" or draw the course on a map. He would try to check the position he had calculated by observing the position of the sun and prominent stars.

Above left is a "caravela latina," with a full lateen rig. Above right is the same ship re-rigged as a "caravela redonda," with a square mainsail and foresail. Bigger caravels like this sometimes had a small fourth mast astern of the mizzen. This was known as the counter-mizzen, or bonaventure.

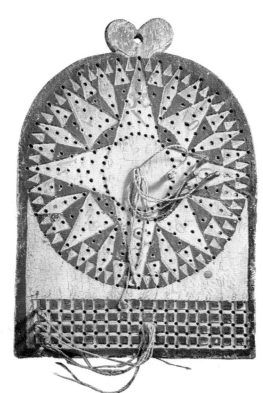

This 16th-century compass (above left), used for figuring out the ship's direction, is set in the cover of a book of maps. As well as north, east, south, and west, the detailed bearings or "points" of the compass are shown. The crew measured time using an hourglass like the one above. They knew that the sand inside took a fixed amount of time to run from the top of the glass to the bottom.

21

THE STATELY CARRACK

I n addition to the caravel, the 15th century also produced the large three- and four-masted cargo ship known as the carrack. Carracks were big enough to be armed with cannons for defense, and eventually developed into the first sailing battleships.

SUPPLY SHIPS

Although caravels were small and fast, they could only carry small amounts of stores and provisions. Therefore it was common to send a supply ship as well on long voyages of exploration. On Columbus's first Atlantic crossing in 1492, the caravels *Pinta* and *Niña* were accompanied by the bigger but clumsier supply ship *Santa Maria*.

A nocturnal, used by early navigators to measure the time by the position of the stars. Accurate ships' clocks, called chronometers, were not available until the 1770s.

By the 1550s, carracks returning to Europe from the Indies carried the richest cargoes afloat. Here the ship on the right has rammed a potentially wealthy victim. It has braved the defender's gunfire to pour a wave of attackers onto the enemy's upper deck.

CARRACKS

Small supply ships, like the *Santa Maria*, were described by the Spanish word *nao*, meaning "ship." But in the later 15th century, bigger, three-masted supply ships were called "carracks," and they remained in use for over a hundred years.

A little nao like the *Santa Maria* might have as few as 40 crewmen. But big trading carracks like the Spanish *San Felipe* needed twice as many sailors, plus soldiers to defend them. When the *San Felipe* was captured sailing home from the East Indies, its cargo of spices, silks, gold, and jewels was worth more than $1.6 million in today's money.

TALL CASTLES

Carracks were tall, ungainly ships, with the rounded bow sweeping up to form a towering forecastle, which supported the foremast. Another lofty castle in the stern carried the mizzenmast, and sometimes a counter-mizzen, too.

Carracks usually carried square sails on the fore- and mainmasts, and lateen sails on the mizzen and counter-mizzen. A new feature of carracks, such as the Portuguese flagship *Santa Caterina do Monte Sinai*, was the rigging of a small "topsail" above the mainsail. This gave more pulling power in tailwinds. The area of sail could also be increased by lacing extra strips, called "bonnets," to the bottom of the square sails. However, with their high castles and many sails, carracks were *very* top-heavy.

FOUR DECKS OR MORE

European carracks were only about half as long as the big Chinese junks, which had just one deck. But the carracks were taller ships, with at least four decks for cargo storage, passenger accommodation, and crew living quarters. Some carracks had as many as six decks, with the extra decks in the high castles.

The deck and mast layout of a big 16th-century carrack. From the bottom, the decks were called the orlop or lower deck (below the waterline); the main deck; and the quarterdeck (astern of the mainmast). There was a short poopdeck above the quarterdeck in the stern, and the tall forecastle usually contained two short decks.

In this painting from about 1520, ships fill Antwerp harbor, one of the leading ports of the 16th century. In the center is a large four-masted carrack with square and lateen sails. A topsail can be seen at the top of its mainmast. To defend their cargoes, carracks carried a wide range of light guns in their castles and upper decks. To the left of the carrack is a galley, widely used by Spain, Venice, and Portugal.

CAGES AND GUNPORTS

Pictures of early 16th century carracks show the upper decks covered with what look like untiled roofs. These "cages" were in fact a defense against enemies trying to get on board, and they could be covered with netting to make boarding even harder. Another feature added to carracks were rows of holes, or gunports, cut through the sides of the castles, through which light cannons could be fired. Later, when carracks were built with ports for heavy guns on the maindeck, a new age of naval warfare began.

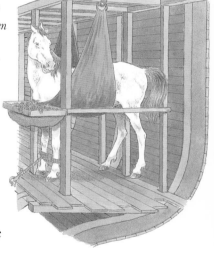

Transporting horses and other livestock by sea was difficult. Rough weather could make them fall and break their legs. This is one of the ways used to secure the animals below decks.

counter-mizzen · mizzenmast · mainmast · foremast · forecastle · bowsprit · poop deck · quarterdeck · cage · main deck · orlop deck

ARMADA GALLEONS

Above is an early naval gun, recovered from the English Mary Rose, sunk in 1545. Its barrel was an iron sheet bent into a tube, strengthened with iron hoops. By the time of the Armada, most big guns were cast in one piece from bronze or iron (right). The powder, charge, and shot were rammed down the barrel through the muzzle.

The increased use of cannons in the 16th century marked the end of a style of naval warfare which originated in the sea battles of Ramesses III in ancient Egypt. Now warships carried powerful guns as well as soldiers who could storm and capture other ships. These guns could even win a sea battle without soldiers becoming directly involved.

THE FIRST BROADSIDES

At first, guns were used to batter the decks of approaching enemy ships. The rows of guns, firing through ports cut in the sides of the ship, became known as "broadsides." The crew shot at the enemy troops to make it easier for their own soldiers to board and capture the other ship. But it was still the soldiers' bows and arrows, spears and swords that won battles.

A one-piece gun, about eight feet long, being recovered from the Spanish Armada ship El Gran Grifon.

GALLEYS AND GALLEASSES

Guns were also useful additions to the oldest of all warships, the oared galley. By the 1540s the use of guns mounted in broadsides, combined with oars for rowing in calm Mediterranean weather, had produced a new type of warship. This was the galleass (top): a galley with three masts and a broadside of light guns above the rowing deck.

An impatient captain looks on as one of his crew receives treatment from the ship's "barber surgeon." Only the biggest warships carried a barber surgeon for treating sickness and wounds, but their treatments were fairly primitive. The large sailcloth bundle contains the body of a dead crewman, sewed up and ready for burial at sea.

GALLEYS AT LEPANTO

The last great battle between fleets of oared warships took place off Greece, at Lepanto, in 1571. A fleet of 208 galleasses and galleys from Spain, Malta, and Venice destroyed a Turkish fleet of 273 galleys. Lepanto seemed to prove that cannon-armed galleys and galleasses were valuable fighting ships—and so they were, against ships of their own type. But the Spanish Armada battles showed that galleasses could not hope to defeat agile sailing ships armed with broadsides, especially in the rougher conditions of the Atlantic.

"GREAT SHIPS" AND GALLEONS

At the time of Lepanto, huge sailing ships of 1,100 tons were being built. But the newest type of sailing warship was the smaller, faster "galleon." Galleon designers thought it was better to use the decks for cannons than to pack them with soldiers. The most famous English galleon, the 492-ton *Revenge*, carried 34 guns. In contrast, Spain's 1,100-ton *San Martin* carried 300 soldiers but only 14 more cannons than the *Revenge*.

In 1588, Spain sent a great "Armada" to escort its army across the English Channel. This resulted in the first battle between fleets of galleons armed with broadsides. The English did not try to board the Spanish ships. Instead, they relied on gunfire, turning their faster galleons to fire one broadside after another. This enabled them to fire twice the weight of shot at the bigger but slower enemy ships.

The Spanish fleet edged up to succor [aid] their galleasses, and so rescued them and the galleon, after which time they were never seen in fight any more, so badly was their entertainment in this encounter.

——— *Lord Howard of Effingham* ———

In the Armada campaign, the English and Spanish fleets had about the same number of ships. But, in four battles, Spain's galleons, great ships, and galleasses never once came to grips with the English fleet, and the invasion was abandoned.

In this painting of an Armada battle, we can see how ships swarmed around their enemies like angry bees. However, the artist has made little distinction between England's low and slim galleons (red crosses on white flags) and Spain's larger ships (yellow crosses on red). In the foreground is a galleass.

Even though the galley (kitchen) fire was enclosed by bricks to prevent sparks from burning the ship, it was only safe to cook when the weather was calm.

EAST INDIAMEN

John Harrison's Chronometer No. 4 was the first timepiece able to keep running on voyages around the world, making navigation much more accurate.

This detailed picture shows East Indiamen of the Dutch East India Company.

Because of the discoveries of its sea captains, Portugal had taken control of the rich sea trade with India and the Far East. However, by 1600 the European sea powers were battling to seize the biggest share of this trade. For the next 250 years, large, well-armed merchant ships known to all seamen as "East Indiamen" carried precious cargoes from the Orient.

THE EAST INDIA COMPANIES

The 17th century saw the founding of the famous "East India Companies"—the English in 1600, the Dutch in 1602, the Danish in 1616, and the French in 1664. The merchants who ran the companies had one main goal: to make profits and wealth through trade. The companies hired their own sailors, soldiers, and well-armed ships to bring home the cargoes—and to fight if necessary.

FOR PEACE OR WAR

The profits from a successful East India voyage ran into millions (the captain of an East Indiaman would earn at least $8,000 per voyage), but the risks and dangers were also high. To help overcome them, a new type of ship was built.

The handsome East Indiamen of the 17th and 18th centuries (above) were really a cross between the heavy trading carracks and the swift fighting galleons of the 16th century. Although they had fewer guns than a warship of the same size, the early ones could carry over 385 tons of cargo. By the late 18th century, European East Indiamen were the finest ships afloat, and their decks could hold over 1,000 tons. They had to be able to carry a very wide range of goods, on both outward and homeward voyages. A typical outward-bound cargo would include gold and silver, iron, lead and copper, cloth and finished clothes, household goods, building bricks, tiles, and barrels of beer, wine, gin, and brandy.

PERILS OF THE VOYAGE

The East Indiamen also carried important passengers to and from the Indies. These people demanded comfortable quarters, so the ships were fitted with luxury cabins.

The almost 10,000 mile voyage around Africa to India took four months, and a trip to China took nearly six. The sailors had to be ready at all times to fight off rivals and pirates. Apart from the risks of shipwreck and casualties in battle, a crew could easily lose a man every 10 days from accidents or disease. So East Indiamen sailed with as many as 250 crewmen and passengers to allow for these losses.

An East Indiaman in a breaming dock (right). Here the massive growths of seaweed and barnacles that built up on a long ocean voyage were burned off. The ship's underside was then scraped clean and the seams between the planks were waterproofed with tar in preparation for the next voyage.

THE LOSS OF THE "WHITE LION"

In 1613, a typical sea battle resulted in the sinking of the 30-gun Dutch East Indiaman *Witte Leeuw* ("White Lion"). Sailing with three other ships, the *Witte Leeuw* was returning from the Indies with a priceless cargo: 1,311 diamonds, a hold full of delicate Chinese porcelain, and over 15,000 bags of pepper, as well as other costly spices. At St. Helena in the South Atlantic, the Dutch ships met two rival Portuguese ships, which they immediately attacked. But the Portuguese fought back. Their gunfire started a blaze that ignited *Witte Leeuw*'s gunpowder and sank the ship and its entire cargo.

The later East Indiamen were so powerfully armed, with broadsides of 50 guns or more, that they were used as battleships in times of war. In February 1804, a convoy of East Indiamen chased away an enemy battle fleet off the coast of Malaya. The battle fleet's admiral retreated because he thought the well-armed East Indiamen were heavy ships of war.

"All at Sea," a cartoon showing after-dinner chaos aboard a storm-tossed East Indiaman. Even the wealthiest passengers in their luxury cabins could not escape from the miseries of rough weather.

Beautiful Chinese porcelain, part of a rich cargo recovered by divers from the wreck of a 17th-century East Indiaman.

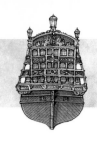

SHIPS OF THE LINE

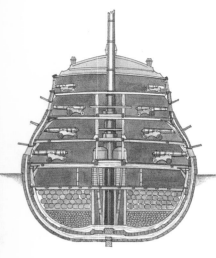

The gun decks of a First Rate, showing the inward slope or "tumble-home" of the sides. The gunpowder was stored safely below the waterline in a "magazine."

After the defeat of the Spanish Armada, warship designers strove to increase the fire-power of the fighting galleon. The result was the heavy sailing warship known as the "ship of the line," with three decks and 100 guns or more.

THREE-DECKED GIANTS

The 1580s galleon carried its guns on the main and quarterdecks. It seemed easy enough to design bigger ships armed with two full decks of guns instead of one. Unfortunately, many of the first "two-deckers" were too narrow and top-heavy. Several capsized, such as the 1,430-ton Swedish *Vasa*, which turned over in the harbor on its maiden voyage in 1628.

The answer to top-heaviness in big ships was to have a hull with a pear-shaped cross-section, with the upper hull sides sloping inward. The heaviest guns were mounted on the lowest deck for stability. This system produced warships which were the biggest and most powerful ships for the next 250 years.

GUNS AND CREW

At this time, guns were named by the weight of shot they fired. A typical "three-decker" would carry 32-pounder guns on the lower gun deck, 24-pounders on the middle deck, and 12-pounders on the upper deck. Other guns were mounted on the quarterdeck and forecastle.

An 80-gun "three-decker" like France's *Bucentaure* would have a crew of about 800 officers and men. On board these ships, conditions were hard. Men had a space less than two feet wide in which to sling their hammocks, and, with fresh food unavailable on long voyages, disease could be as life-threatening as enemy shots.

Action on the upper deck. The gun crew have just reloaded and run out the gun using ropes and pulleys. They are now aiming it for the next broadside. To the left, a soldier is firing his musket at troops in an enemy ship's rigging.

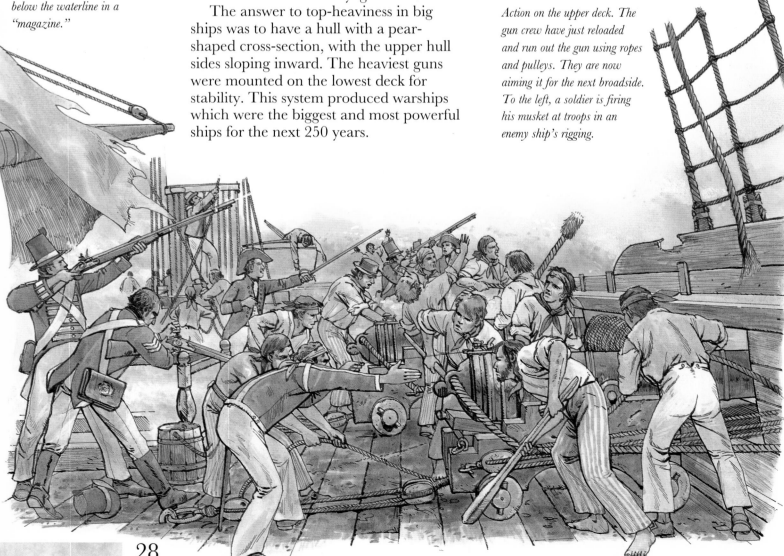

THE LINE OF BATTLE

By the late 17th century, ships no longer fought individual battles at sea. Instead, admirals used their broadsides by sailing their ships in a formation known as the "line of battle." The lines of ships would sail past each other less than 550 yards apart, their guns pounding the enemy.

Only the most powerful warships were considered fit for the line of battle. These heavy sailing battleships became known as "ships of the line," and were graded or "rated" by the number of guns they carried. First Rates had 100 guns or more, Second Rates 84–100, Third Rates 70–84, and Fourth Rates 50–70 guns. By the 1790s, Fifth Rates (32–50 guns) were no longer considered fit for the line of battle.

THE MIGHTY *SANTISSIMA*

During the 1760s, France began to strengthen its navy. As well as building fast and powerful ships, the French navy paid special attention to improving its gunnery. Moreover, France and Spain built bigger First Rates than their greatest rival, Britain, and armed them with heavier guns (36- and 48-pounders). The biggest First Rate of all was Spain's four-decked *Santissima Trinidad* with 136 guns. Like many First Rate ships of the line, the *Santissima* had a thick oak hull that could withstand all but the heaviest broadside.

Britain's response to powerful ships like the *Santissima* was to train its gun crews until they could fire at least three broadsides to the enemy's two. The ships would try to cut across the enemy's bow or stern and "rake" it—firing broadsides that smashed from one end of the ship to the other. Just one "raking" broadside could inflict terrible damage. This was the fate of the *Santissima Trinidad* in the Battle of Trafalgar in 1805. The 98-gun British *Neptune* got under *Santissima*'s stern and raked it repeatedly until it surrendered. The *Santissima* was so badly damaged that it later sank.

Although they were built for war, some ships of the line were beautifully decorated. In this Dutch painting of a battle in 1666, the gilded carving, called "gingerbread," can be seen on the stern and hull sides.

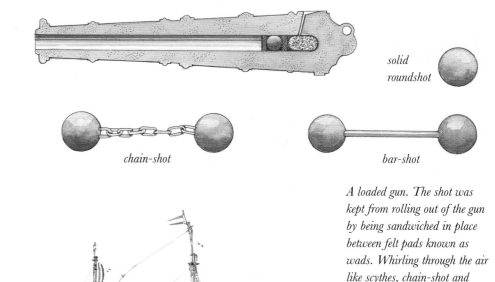

solid
roundshot

chain-shot

bar-shot

A loaded gun. The shot was kept from rolling out of the gun by being sandwiched in place between felt pads known as wads. Whirling through the air like scythes, chain-shot and bar-shot were used to disable enemy ships by slicing their rigging to pieces.

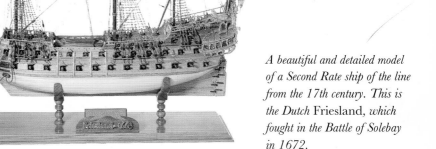

A beautiful and detailed model of a Second Rate ship of the line from the 17th century. This is the Dutch Friesland, *which fought in the Battle of Solebay in 1672.*

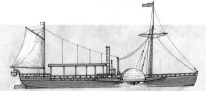

The large passenger-carrying steamships had much better facilities than the wooden sailing ships that preceded them. This is a glazed toilet from the Great Britain, a luxury unknown on early warships.

Ten years after the Battle of Trafalgar, the world's first ships powered by steam engines were in service. These were small tugboats driven by paddle-wheels. Over the next 30 years, the first ocean crossings were made using steam power, and the first ships were built with iron frames and plating instead of wood.

STEAM GOES AFLOAT

The first steam-powered ships of practical use were the 56-foot, single-paddle tugboat *Charlotte Dundas* in Scotland, built in 1802, and the larger, twin-paddle *Clermont* in America, built in 1807. The *Clermont*, pictured above right, was the first steamboat to carry passengers. However, it was 40 years before steam engines were able to provide enough power for oceangoing ships. Even then, steamships were given a full rig of sails in case the machinery broke down.

FULL STEAM AHEAD

By the 1840s, steam-powered ships were advanced enough to ensure that freight deliveries and passengers arrived on time, whatever the wind and weather. At the same time, industry was now able to forge heavy girders, cast machine parts, and roll strong plates. This meant that ships could be made completely of iron, and could be built much bigger and stronger than was possible with wood. And with an iron hull there was less risk of fires caused by the engine furnaces and funnel sparks. For shipowners, bigger ships meant larger cargoes, more passengers, and bigger profits.

A day of glory: Great Britain *is towed downriver to begin its first transatlantic crossing in 1845, which was made in just under 15 days. During its three-week stay in New York,* Great Britain *earned the owners an extra $250 each day, as 1,000 admiring visitors paid 25 cents each to tour the ship.*

BRUNEL'S *GREAT BRITAIN*

These great advances in shipbuilding were typified by the *Great Britain*, designed in 1845 by Isambard Kingdom Brunel.

With a length of over 320 feet and weighing over 4,000 tons, the *Great Britain* was the first big iron ship ever built. It was also the first oceangoing steamship to rely on a stern propeller instead of big side paddlewheels. This propeller had six blades and measured 16 feet across—bigger than any propeller built before. On the ship's trial run, the *Great Britain*'s engines drove it at 11 knots (about 11 miles per hour). Brunel also designed a streamlined, balanced rudder (instead of using the traditional rudder like a hinged plate), to make the ship easier to steer. This new type of rudder and the six-bladed propeller are still used on ships today.

ALL FOR PASSENGER COMFORT

The *Great Britain* was designed to make fast and comfortable Atlantic crossings. It was fitted with special keels to make it roll less in rough weather. This made traveling more comfortable for the passengers. The ship had 26 single- and 113 double-passenger cabins, and its hull had several watertight compartments. It was the biggest, safest passenger-carrying ship since the giant Chinese junks of over 500 years earlier. The *Great Britain* served from 1845 to 1886, when it was abandoned in the Falkland Islands.

Passengers admire the spacious interior of the Great Britain. *It was the first ship designed and built specifically as a luxury liner.*

Some of the more unusual designs for ships' propellers, which are known as screws.

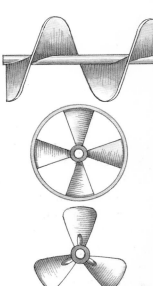

SUBMARINE ATTACK!

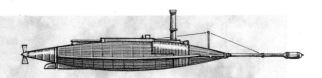

In 1776, American colonists trying to win their freedom from Britain lacked ships big enough to attack the British navy blockading New York. So an American named David Bushnell built an underwater craft—named *Turtle*—which made the first submarine attack in naval history.

BUSHNELL'S *TURTLE*

Bushnell's *Turtle* looked like a wooden egg. It could dive and surface by filling and emptying tanks with water and was driven by a hand-cranked propeller. It carried an explosive charge for attaching to its target. *Turtle* was used only once, in an attack on the British ship *Eagle* in August 1776. The craft worked exactly as designed, but its crewman could not attach the explosive charge to the *Eagle* because of copper sheeting that protected the underside from seaworms and seaweed.

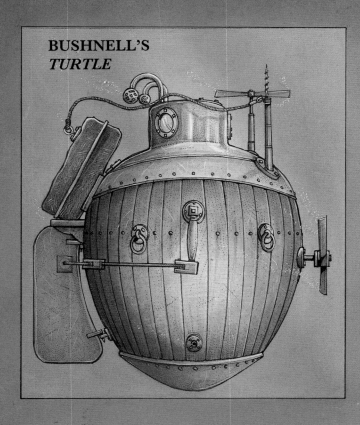

BUSHNELL'S
TURTLE

1 Water ballast tank
2 Propeller
3 Screw for attaching charge to underside of ship
4 Explosive charge attached to screw
5 Breathing tube
6 Steering gear

THE SOUTHERN "DAVIDS"

When the American Civil War broke out in 1861, the Confederate South used craft called "Davids" to fight the powerful fleet of the northern Union states. These cigar-shaped craft could submerge just below the surface. They were armed with a "spar torpedo," an explosive charge held out on a long pole. Some "Davids" (above left) had a small steam engine, but most were powered by an eight-man crew turning a long shaft.

The "Davids" were submersibles. They could not dive deeply, but were weighted to run just below the surface, in calm water only—a rough sea would flood and sink them. The eight human pistons of the "David" *H. L. Hunley*, sweating at their long crankshaft in increasingly bad air, had to crouch with their backs against the submersible's curved sides.

THE "DAVIDS" ATTACK

The original *David*, so-named because it seemed like a tiny David attacking the enemy's huge Goliath, was steam-powered, with a three-man crew. On the night of October 5, 1863, *David* steamed out to attack *New Ironsides*, the most powerful ship in the Union fleet. When the *David*'s torpedo exploded on *New Ironsides*'s waterline, the Union ship was saved only by its armor plating.

The second "David" attack was made by the man-powered *H. L. Hunley* on the night of February 17, 1864. A small raised hatch enabled the commander to see where he was going. *Hunley*'s torpedo blew a huge hole in the Union's wooden warship *Housatonic*—the first ship ever sunk by a submarine. But the explosion also swamped and sank the *Hunley*, drowning all of the crew.

The Confederate submersible H. L. Hunley makes its attack on the Housatonic, its spar torpedo pointing forward. Turn over the see-through page to see inside the Hunley. The air is getting hotter and sweatier as the crew work to drive the Hunley through the water. The box on the opposite page shows David Bushnell's Turtle. Both the Hunley and the Turtle made their attacks at night, moving just below the surface.

1 Spar torpedo
2 "Diving plane" to keep craft just below surface
3 Wheel for steering
4 Commander
5 Pump and ballast tank
6 Crankshaft
7 Rudder

THE NEW IRONCLADS

By the 1850s, wooden warships faced a new threat: guns firing explosive shells instead of solid shot. Against the bursting power of these shells, ships had only one protection—armor plating. The age of a new breed of warship, the steam-driven "ironclad," had begun.

BELTS OF ARMOR

The world's first ironclads were the French *Gloire* and the British *Warrior*. The *Gloire* (above right), launched in 1859, was the first warship to be given special protection from shellfire. The *Gloire* was a wooden steam frigate with a "belt" of armored plates around its waterline to protect the engine room and guns. The *Warrior*, launched in 1860, was the first steam warship built completely of iron. The *Warrior* was given additional protection by armor plates four inches thick, reinforced by 17 inches of very hard teak wood.

This cross-section of an early ironclad shows the engines located below the waterline, the uptake for a funnel at the center, and a belt of armor (iron plate backed by teak wood) protecting the center of the ship above the waterline.

A sweating gun crew, stripped to the waist, work in the turret of the American ironclad Marblehead *during the Spanish-American War of 1898. The curved rail used for "training" the gun from side to side can be seen.*

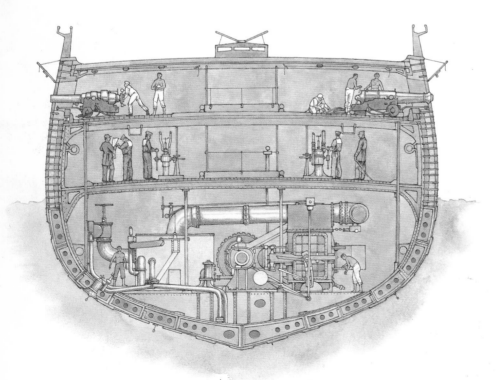

IRONCLADS IN BATTLE

Ironclads proved their resilience under fire during the American Civil War. The Confederates, facing the much larger Union navy, salvaged an abandoned wooden steam-powered frigate, the *Merrimack*, and armed and plated its hull. In March 1862, in its first battle, the *Merrimack* sank one frigate by ramming and caused another to run aground.

The next day the *Merrimack* was challenged by the Union *Monitor*. The *Merrimack* had 10 guns to *Monitor*'s two, but *Monitor*'s guns were mounted in a rotating turret, not in fixed broadsides. The two ironclads battered each other at point-blank range for nearly three hours, but neither could seriously damage the other.

SINKING BY RAMMING

As well as proving that armor protected ships, the *Merrimack* seemed to teach another lesson. This was that a steam-powered ironclad could use one of the oldest tactics in naval warfare: ramming enemy ships to sink them. From then on, all new ironclads were given a pointed and armored bow for ramming. However, very few ships were ever sunk by ramming.

THE TURRET-RAM *BUFFEL*

By 1868, ships like the *Buffel* ("Buffalo"), built for the Dutch navy, were being produced. The Dutch wanted their new warship to have all the important features proved in battle since 1862—armored protection, guns mounted in a turret instead of in fixed broadsides, and an armored bow for ramming. With neither gun-decks nor sails, *Buffel* looked nothing like the first ironclads launched only eight years before.

ATTACK AND DEFENSE

Apart from the menacing curve of her armored ram, *Buffel*'s "teeth" were two stubby guns that fired explosive shells nine inches in diameter. The guns were mounted in a low circular turret protected by eight inches of armor plate backed by 11 inches of hard teak. *Buffel*'s armored belt was strongest where it protected the boilers and engines near the center of the ship. This protection extended three feet above and below the waterline. *Buffel* was one of the first ships to have twin screw propellers, its engines providing a top speed of just under 13 knots. It carried a crew of 102 officers and men.

The first battle between ironclads took place in March 1862. The tiny Monitor *(in the foreground) was described by one spectator as looking "like a tin can on a plank."*

Built only six years after the Merrimack *and* Monitor, *the Dutch ironclad* Buffel *had a central turret armed with two heavy guns.*

THE CLIPPER YEARS

Some of the main clipper routes and cargoes—immigrants to California, tea from China, and wool from Australia.

California clippers
1840s–1850s

China tea clippers
1860s–1870s

Australia wool clippers
1870s–1890s

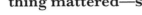

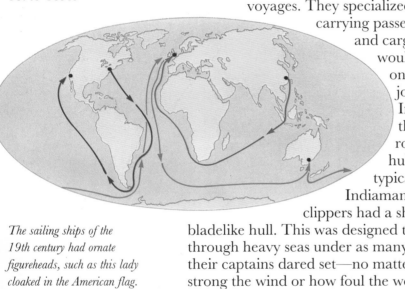

The sailing ships of the 19th century had ornate figureheads, such as this lady cloaked in the American flag.

The famous clippers were the fastest and the most beautiful sailing ships ever built. For the clippers, whose great years lasted from the 1840s to the 1880s, only one thing mattered—speed.

BUILT FOR SPEED

To compete with steamships, clippers were built to make fast long-distance voyages. They specialized in carrying passengers, and cargoes that would perish on longer journeys. Instead of the sturdy rounded hull of a typical East Indiaman, the clippers had a sharp, bladelike hull. This was designed to slice through heavy seas under as many sails as their captains dared set—no matter how strong the wind or how foul the weather. With 32,250 square feet of canvas and driven at speeds up to 17 knots, clippers were the fastest ships ever to rely on sail alone.

THE CALIFORNIA CLIPPERS

The first and fastest clippers were American-built ships that carried immigrants seeking gold to California (1848) and Australia (1850). The distance from New York to California (around Cape Horn) was about the same as that from London to Melbourne—19,000 miles. The fastest clippers of the 1850s could cover the distance in 65 days.

Journey's end, and the first clippers home unload the highly prized pick of the Chinese tea crop.

THE TEA CLIPPERS

In contrast to the emigrant clippers, the tea clippers did not carry passengers. Their cargoes of tea from China were sealed to keep out the water that frequently swept the decks. In a hard-driven clipper, the crew (30 or less of the toughest seamen of all time) often went without hot food for days because it was too rough to light the galley fire. In such conditions, a man who fell overboard stood little chance of surviving.

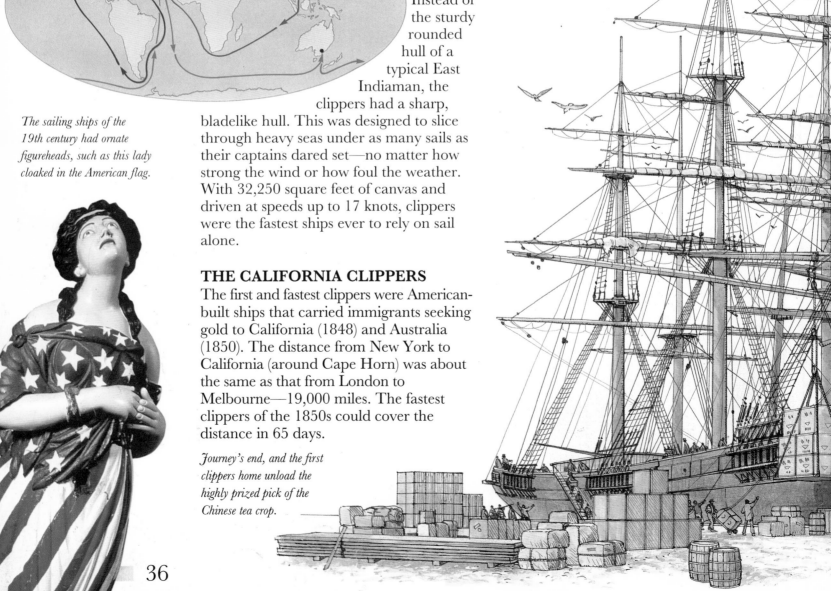

THE GREAT CLIPPER RACES

By the mid-19th century, clippers from many countries were carrying passengers and mining equipment to California and Australia. In the 1860s, every clipper owner dreamed of winning the prestigious race to bring the first tea cargo of each year from China to London.

In 1866 the most dramatic of the tea clipper races took place between *Ariel*, *Taeping*, and *Serica*. All three sailed from the great China tea port of Foochow within minutes of each other on May 30. After 99 days of racing over 20,000 miles, *Taeping* docked at London at 9:45 P.M. on September 6, followed by *Ariel* at 10:15, and *Serica* at 11:45!

TRADE WITH AUSTRALIA

Even these splendid voyages could not win back the world's ocean trade from steam. The days of the China clippers ended with the opening of the Suez Canal in 1869. The new canal enabled the coal-hungry steamships to take a shorter route through the Mediterranean Sea instead of around Africa. Previously, they had been forced to make several expensive stops to refuel.

Some large clippers were able to survive by trading with South America and Australia, partly because there were too few coaling stations on the route. In the 1880s, ships such as the *Cutty Sark* were able to bring wool from Australia to London in about two months. But even huge ships like Germany's 5,500-ton, five-masted *Preussen*, launched in 1902, could not halt the steamship's progress.

The great clouds of canvas gracing clippers under full sail were favorite subjects of artists. This is the American giant, Sovereign of the Seas. Sovereign *set an all-time sailing record of 13 days, 14 hours from New York to Liverpool, at times reaching the incredible speed (for a sailing ship) of 22 knots.*

Aboard an American immigrant clipper, a passenger has broken the rules and tried to climb the rigging. He has been caught and tied there by crewmen, and not released until he has bought his freedom with a bottle of rum!

DREADNOUGHTS

Early in the 20th century, the most powerful warships were the dreadnoughts. Encased in steel armor and armed with turret-mounted heavy guns with a range of 16 miles or more, the dreadnoughts were the costliest and most destructive weapon that the world had ever seen.

THE TORPEDO THREAT

Beginning in the 1870s, new weapons and new inventions forced dramatic changes in warship design. Sails and masts vanished, as engines improved and more coal could be carried. There was also a deadly new naval weapon, the self-propelled torpedo, which ran underwater before exploding against the hull of a ship. Designers now had to install more guns in turrets so they could be aimed at these fast-moving, torpedo-firing ships (above right).

A COMBINATION OF GUNS

By 1900, battleships no longer carried the largest possible number of heavy guns, as in the days of sail. Instead they were armed with light guns. These were easier to aim at small, fast torpedo-boats that fired their torpedoes at close range. In 1905, a typical battleship was armed with 12 or more light "quick-firers." Most of these guns did not have the power or the range to sink the enemy's biggest ships.

Britain's Dreadnought *at sea in 1906. The slanting booms along the sides could be swung out to support heavy nets, designed to protect the ship from torpedo attack.*

FISHER'S *DREADNOUGHT*

When Admiral Fisher became chief of the British navy in 1904, he ordered the building of a new type of battleship. The *Dreadnought* was completed in 1906 after only 14 months, and was the first "all big-gun" battleship. The ship's ten 12-inch guns could fire twice as many heavy shells as any other ship afloat, with a range of almost 50,000 feet. These guns could fire up to 30 times farther than the guns of the early 19th-century ships.

The *Dreadnought* was powered by new steam turbine engines driving four screws. This enabled it to steam at over 20 knots. The *Dreadnought* was also heavily protected, with an armor belt 11 inches thick. In total, it displaced over 19,800 tons—20 times more than most Armada galleons.

NEW BUILDING

The *Dreadnought* gave Britain an important technological lead over its most powerful naval rival, Germany. However, this meant that all older battleships had to be replaced. Now countries such as Germany, France, Japan, and the U.S. had a chance to build large fleets of modern dreadnoughts to rival Britain's.

By the time World War I broke out in August 1914, new "super-dreadnoughts" were being built. These weighed as much as 36,850 tons and carried eight 15-inch guns. By using oil fuel, which burned more cleanly and was much easier to store than coal, these new dreadnoughts could reach a speed of 25 knots.

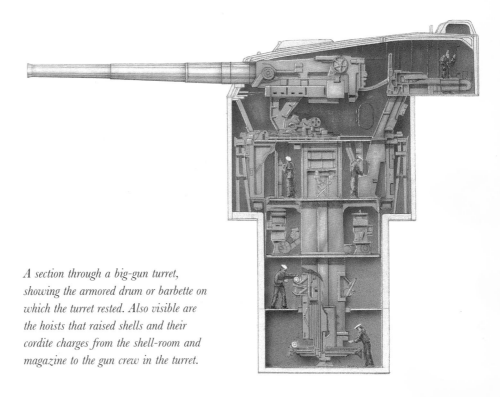

A section through a big-gun turret, showing the armored drum or barbette on which the turret rested. Also visible are the hoists that raised shells and their cordite charges from the shell-room and magazine to the gun crew in the turret.

THE BATTLE OF JUTLAND

The only battle between the British and German dreadnought fleets took place off Jutland, Denmark, on May 31, 1916. It was the biggest battleship fight of the 20th century, with 16 German dreadnoughts ranged against 28 British. Both fleets, fearing torpedo attacks, stayed at long range. The British fleet lost more ships than the German fleet, but the latter returned to port and never again risked a major battle. Although battleships saw action in World War II, control of the sea had passed to aircraft carriers and submarines.

In the 1980s, the United States navy took two of its old battleships from storage and gave them a new lease on life by equipping them with cruise missiles. Cruise missiles can hit a target hundreds of miles away with great accuracy. The battleships kept their huge 16-inch guns, which are being fired in this dramatic picture. They are unlikely ever to be fired at enemy ships, but have been used to bombard targets on land.

The main picture shows the Normandie. *Renowned for its spacious design, the liner's interior was decorated by some of France's finest artists. The panel below is typical of the many striking scenes on the ship. You can turn over the see-through page to look inside the* Normandie, *and into one of the twin-berth staterooms.* Normandie's *passenger facilities were the most luxurious afloat. Equipped to outclass the world's finest hotels, all first-class rooms included a telephone and a private bath or shower.*

By 1900 the passenger shipping lines of Europe and America were competing to provide the fastest, most luxurious passenger service across the North Atlantic. The race was on for the "Blue Riband of the Atlantic," awarded to the liner making the quickest crossing.

THE LOVELY *NORMANDIE*

France's *Normandie* was designed to be the biggest, fastest, and most beautiful liner in the world. When it entered service in May 1935, the *Normandie* caused a sensation. From a high flaring bow—designed to prevent waves breaking over the deck—beautiful lines swept gracefully back to an elegantly curved stern.

BUILT FOR LUXURY

The *Normandie* was built to provide 1,975 passengers with the ultimate in high-speed luxury and elegance while crossing the Atlantic. In addition to 300 crew members, there were nearly 1,000 domestic staff to provide services as good as any hotel on shore.

The *Normandie* had the most modern engines available. Steam from oil-fired boilers drove four electric motors, each one connected to a separate propeller shaft. Using about 5,500 tons of oil per transatlantic crossing, *Normandie* could steam at up to 32 knots.

1 **First-class staterooms and cabins**
2 **Tourist-class accommodation**
3 **First-class Dining Saloon**
4 **Grand salon (first-class lounge)**
5 **Theater (with children's playroom above, under funnel)**
6 **Chapel**
7 **Swimming pool**
8 **Crew's quarters**

SPACE AND BEAUTY

The *Normandie* was also remarkable for the huge areas of open deck space that provided an unbroken sweep of the ship. The mighty hull held 13 levels, from the upper sun deck to the "H" deck far below the waterline. The superb first-class dining room was longer than the famous "Hall of Mirrors" in France's Palace of Versailles, and there was even a separate dining room for passengers' servants. The finest artists and decorators made the *Normandie* a showcase of French art in the 1930s, with an attention to detail seen in no other ship. The *Normandie* was famed for its beautiful colored glass, used for wall decoration as well as lighting.

The *Normandie* fulfilled all hopes by winning the Blue Riband on its maiden voyage with a speed of 29.98 knots. Sadly, while marooned in New York by the outbreak of World War II, it was destroyed by fire and sunk in 1942.

Always the showpiece of the luxury liner, the first-class dining room (left) broke all previous records in size, beauty, and grandeur. During the afternoon, first-class passengers could have refreshments and dance in the Grand salon (below), where balls and concerts were held after dinner. Children were entertained in the children's theater and playroom (bottom). Children crossing in the Normandie *were well cared for and the attention given to their entertainment made it possible for their parents to enjoy themselves completely.*

9   **Garage on "G" deck**
10 **Ship's stores**
11 **Cargo hold on "H" deck**
12 **Boilers**
13 **Electric motors (turbines)**
14 **Kitchens**

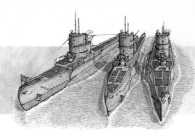

THE DEADLY U-BOATS

The special "Submarine War Badge," awarded only to the U-boat crewmen of the German navy (Kriegsmarine).

A section through a German Type VII U-boat. Astern of the central control room are the diesel engines used on the surface, and the electric motors used when running submerged. A torpedo has just been fired, and the captain has turned his periscope to look for another target.

In both World Wars, the torpedo-firing submarine was found to be a deadly weapon against every form of surface ship. Victory or defeat could depend on the ability of ships to survive against fleets of enemy submarines.

THE DEADLY U-BOAT

In 1898, American inventor John Holland built the first practical submarine. But it was the German U-boat—from the German word *unterseeboot* or "undersea boat"—that proved the submarine could be an effective weapon. From the outbreak of World War I in 1914, U-boats threatened the much bigger battleship fleets of Britain and France. But the German High Command also used U-boats to sink over *11 million tons* of supplies that its enemy's war effort depended on. The most successful U-boat of all, *U-35*, sank an amazing 224 supply ships between 1914 and 1918.

By the spring of 1917, victory for the U-boats seemed in sight, but the Allies found the answer just in time. By sailing the merchant ships in groups called convoys, protected by an escort of warships, they greatly reduced their losses.

These are the cramped conditions in which crews lived and worked. They stood no chance if the U-boat's watertight hull was cracked by depth charges. Until the invention of nuclear power, submarines had to surface often to recharge their electric batteries using their air-breathing diesel engines.

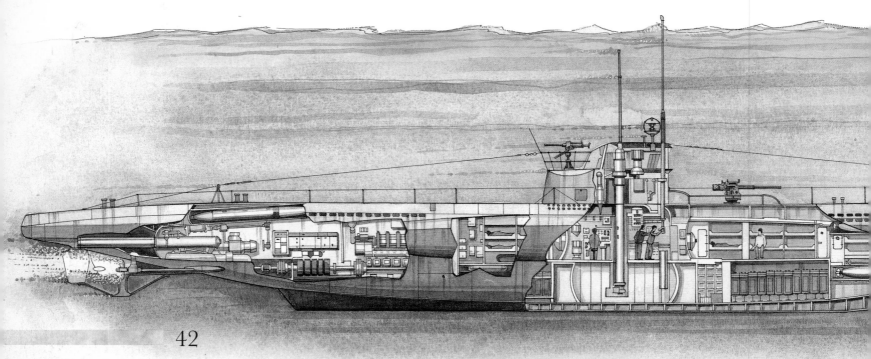

THE TYPE VII U-BOAT

During World War II, the Allies again faced the U-boat threat. The main U-boat used by the German navy was called the Type VII. A typical Type VII U-boat was 220 feet long, and displaced 859 tons on the surface—973 tons when submerged with its tanks flooded.

The Type VII's deadly armament was its 14 torpedoes, each of which could sink a large merchant ship. The torpedoes could be fired from four torpedo tubes in the bow and another one in the stern. A typical Type VII also carried a powerful three-inch gun and three light anti-aircraft guns in case it had to fight on the surface.

A DANGEROUS LIFE

Life for a U-boat's 44 officers and men was extremely uncomfortable and hazardous. When close to their enemy, they often had to remain submerged for hours on end. There was often a shortage of oxygen, as poisonous fumes from the U-boat's diesel engines built up in the cramped quarters.

In addition, by 1939 the British and French had found a way of detecting a submerged U-boat. This was by using sonar (SOund Navigation And Ranging). Sonar sent out a sound pulse which returned an echo or "ping" when it hit the hull of any nearby U-boat. The U-boat hunter would then try to sail over the U-boat and drop "depth-charges." These were bombs set to explode at the U-boat's estimated depth.

Members of the crew welcomed any opportunity to go on deck. The U-boat would be vulnerable while on the surface, so lookouts stood on the conning tower (left) to watch out for enemy ships and aircraft.

A photograph of a merchant ship under attack, taken through a U-boat's periscope. Submarine captains tried to show as little of the periscope as possible, to avoid being spotted by enemy aircraft and warships.

BATTLE OF THE ATLANTIC

Even with sonar and other electronic devices for hunting U-boats, Britain, and later the U.S., came very close to defeat in the "Battle of the Atlantic" (1940–1943). "Wolf packs" of U-boats attacked convoys crossing the Atlantic, inflicting terrible losses. Skillful U-boat captains could avoid sonar by getting inside the convoy and attacking on the surface at night, when the small outline of the U-boat's conning tower was almost impossible to see.

A DEADLY GAME

When a U-boat was detected, the escorting warships played a deadly game of cat-and-mouse, trying to destroy the submarine or drive it away from the convoy.

Despite their skill, the U-boats could not win the war at sea. Between 1939 and 1945, 1,162 new U-boats entered service. Of these, only 156 survived the war. All the rest had been sunk, lost by accident or shipwreck, or scuttled—sunk by their own crews rather than surrendering to the Allies.

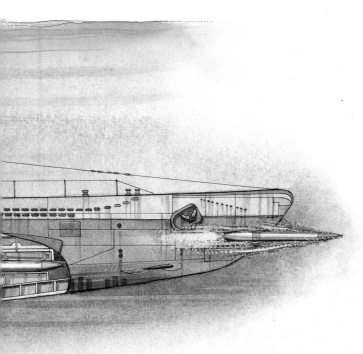

SUPER CARRIERS

U ntil the 1950s, the 88,000-ton luxury liners remained the biggest ships ever built. But with the coming of nuclear power, these pre-war ships were surpassed by the huge nuclear-powered aircraft carriers of the United States navy. These great vessels can travel around the world without refueling.

An F-14 Tomcat fighter, armed with underwing missiles, is hurled into the air from the bow steam catapult of an American "Nimitz" class super carrier.

THE FIRST "FLAT-TOPS"

The first aircraft carriers appeared at the end of World War I. Rebuilt from the hulls of large merchant ships and battleships, they were designed with a long flight deck from which aircraft could take off and land. However, it was not until World War II that aircraft carriers proved their worth as their planes launched devastating attacks on enemy fleets. During the war in the Pacific, Japanese and American carriers fought intense battles without ever seeing the other's ships!

THE *NIMITZ*

More recently, the United States navy built the USS *Nimitz* and several sister ships. These giant nuclear-powered carriers are the biggest warships (some are over 20 stories high) and the most sophisticated floating structures ever built. (They are surpassed in size only by the oil-carrying super tankers, which displace over 275,000 tons when fully loaded.) The super carriers provide the U.S. navy with floating airfields everywhere they go. The carriers are also complicated floating cities, crammed from end to end with up-to-the-minute technology, including two nuclear reactors that can provide power for at least 13 years. The carriers displace over 100,000 tons and have a crew of 6,300 men and women, 3,000 of whom belong to the "air group" on the ship.

POWER AND GLORY

A carrier's air group operates over 90 aircraft. These include powerful strike aircraft, capable of bombing an enemy's forces by day or night and in nearly all weather. There are also fighters and anti-submarine aircraft for the ship's own protection, "tankers" that can refuel other aircraft in the air, and even electronic warfare aircraft for jamming enemy radar and detecting attackers.

The heavy jets need long flight decks for takeoff and landing. To help them get into the air, giant catapults harness the power of the nuclear reactors and accelerate the jets to over 62 miles per hour in just three seconds. After a flight, aircraft are moved from the flight deck to the giant hangars and workshops below using four elevators at the ship's side. This is a far cry from the tied-up bundles of reeds that ancient Egyptians used as boats!

A MINI CITY

A super carrier generates enough power to supply a city of two million people with electricity, while its crew consumes over 13 tons of food each day! Every year the medical department will complete more than 8,000 blood tests and 3,000 medical checkups.

The scene in the Carrier Air Traffic Control Center (CATCC) of a super carrier. The constantly updated information on the screens shows which aircraft have been launched and which are due for launching or recovery.

Too valuable to sail alone, modern carriers usually operate as part of a battle group. With this carrier are an anti-submarine frigate (upper left) and an anti-aircraft cruiser armed with the AEGIS missile system. AEGIS can engage many targets simultaneously and control an entire fleet's defenses. Radar-fitted aircraft detect low-flying enemy aircraft, while a helicopter is ready to rescue aircrew in the event of a crash at sea.

KEY DATES AND GLOSSARY

Strictly defined, a ship is a sailing vessel with at least three masts. Such craft (with the exception of the giant Chinese junks) did not exist before the 15th century A.D., yet sailors had been making ocean voyages for well over 4,000 years before then. This book uses the word *ship* for vessels able to make cargo-carrying voyages on the open sea. A submarine is any powered vessel capable of diving and returning to the surface.

c2300 B.C. Egyptian fleet attacks Syria, the earliest known use of ships in war.
c1000–550 B.C. Phoenician merchant ships dominate Mediterranean sea trade.
480 B.C. A Greek trireme fleet defeats Persians at the huge battle of Salamis.
264–241 B.C. Roman fleets win control of western Mediterranean from Carthage.
30 B.C.–A.D. 410 The Roman empire is served by world's biggest merchant fleet.
c300–900 Pacific islanders in sailing canoes populate central Pacific islands.
c850–1000 Viking explorers reach Iceland, Greenland, and North America.
c900–1500 Arab traders reach India, the East Indies, and the China coast.

c1480–1500 Portuguese and Spanish caravels open the ocean routes to India and the Americas.
1571 Battle of Lepanto, the last big sea battle between fleets of war galleys.
1588 The Spanish Armada battles, the first sea fights between galleon fleets armed with broadside-mounted cannons.
1808 Fulton's *Phoenix* makes the first sea voyage under steam.
1845 Brunel's *Great Britain* is the first steamship built entirely of iron.
1862 *Merrimack* versus *Monitor*, the first fight between steam-powered "ironclads."
1864 *Housatonic* becomes the first warship to be sunk by submarine attack.
c1848–1880 Record sailing voyages by high-speed clippers fail to stop the transition from sail to steam.
1916 Battle of Jutland, only big sea fight between fleets of dreadnought battleships.
1907–1939 Pursuing the "Blue Riband," fast Atlantic passenger liners become the world's biggest ships.
1940–1943 Germany's U-boats are defeated in the Battle of the Atlantic.
1955 USS *Nautilus*, the first nuclear-powered submarine, enters service.
1975 *Nimitz*, the biggest nuclear-powered warship in history, enters service.

Roman soldiers rush from their galley across a corvus, or "crow," that has been dropped onto an opponent's deck. The large spike on the corvus will hold the ships together. In the background, another oared galley is approaching. In early Greek and Roman times, the job of the rower was considered an honorable one. Later, criminals and slaves were forced to row the galleys.

Glossary

bank: a deck of rowers in a galley.
beam: the width of a ship.
carvel: a shipbuilding technique with the hull planks laid smooth, edge to edge.
clinker: a shipbuilding technique with the hull planks overlapping.
complement: the full number of officers and sailors making up a ship's crew.
convoy: a group of merchant ships sailing together for greater protection.
displacement: a ship's weight in tons, measured by the amount of water pushed aside when the ship is afloat.
galleass: a 16th-century warship driven by both sail and oars.
galley: a warship driven by one or more banks of oars; or a ship's kitchen.
jibs: small triangular sails set at the bow of a ship.
junk: a large Chinese sailing ship, from the Portuguese word *junco* (in turn a version of the Javanese *djong*, or "ship").
lateen sail: a triangular sail perfected by the Arabs and adopted by Europeans, or "Latins" by the 15th century.
poop deck: the small uppermost deck at the stern of a ship.
quarterdeck: a raised deck running from a ship's mainmast to the stern.

tacking: steering a zigzag course to make progress against the wind.
trireme: a Greek war galley driven by three banks of oars.
wa'a kaulua: "double canoe"—a large twin-hulled sailing canoe of the Pacific.

Quotations

The words of navigator Mau Piailug were spoken to the crew of *Hokule'a* before their voyage from Hawaii to Tahiti in 1976. "King Harald's Saga," in praise of Harald Hardraada of Norway, tells of Harald's voyage to Constantinople (Byzantium). Marco Polo's description of Chinese junks comes from his famous travel book, *Description of the World.* Christopher Columbus tells of *Pinta*'s historic landfall in the Americas in the journal of his first Atlantic crossing in 1492. Lord Howard of Effingham was the English fleet's commander during the Spanish Armada campaign. He describes how his galleons drove back the Spanish Armada's galleasses off the Isle of Wight.

INDEX